AI for Beginners
A Step-by-Step Guide for the 60+ Crowd

AI for Beginners: A Step-by-Step Guide for the 60+ Crowd

1. **Introduction to AI (Artificial Intelligence)**
   - Definition of AI in simple terms
   - How AI impacts daily life: examples (smartphones, smart home devices, etc.)
   - Overview of the benefits of AI for seniors
2. **Understanding Basic AI Terms and Concepts**
   - Machine learning, deep learning, chatbots, and virtual assistants
   - Real-life examples of these terms (like Alexa, Google Assistant, Siri)
   - Simplified explanation of how these technologies work behind the scenes
3. **Getting Started with AI: Devices and Applications**
   - The types of devices that use AI (smartphones, tablets, computers)
   - How to check if your current device supports AI applications.
   - Basics of setting up AI on devices (turning on voice assistants, etc.)
4. **Voice Assistants: Your Personal AI Helpers**
   - Introduction to voice assistants (Google Assistant, Siri, Alexa)
   - Step-by-step guide to setting up and using voice assistants on smartphones or smart speakers.
   - Common commands and how to use them for everyday tasks (setting reminders, asking questions)
5. **Using AI for Communication**
   - How AI enhances communication (translating languages, voice typing, etc.)
   - Practical steps to use AI-driven apps for video calls (Zoom, Google Meet, etc.)

o   Tips for using chatbots and virtual assistants for customer service and help.

6. **Staying Organized with AI: Calendars, Reminders, and More**
   o   Setting up reminders, calendar events, and to-do lists using AI
   o   How to use AI apps like Google Keep or Evernote for notetaking
   o   Integrating AI into daily routines to stay organized.

7. **Health and Fitness Tracking with AI**
   o   Overview of AI-powered health and fitness apps (Fitbit, Apple Health)
   o   Step-by-step guide to setting up health apps on smartphones or wearables
   o   Using AI to track medication, exercise routines, and more

8. **Entertainment: Music, Movies, and Books with AI**
   o   How AI recommends content on streaming platforms (Netflix, Spotify)
   o   Step-by-step guide to using AI for finding movies, music, and audiobooks
   o   Using AI to create personalized playlists and recommendations

9. **Smart Home Devices: Making Life Easier with AI**
   o   Introduction to smart home technology (smart lights, thermostats, security cameras)
   o   Setting up and using smart home devices step-by-step
   o   Practical examples of how smart home tech can simplify everyday tasks

10. **Shopping Online Safely with AI**
   o   Using AI for online shopping (personalized suggestions, voice shopping with Alexa)
   o   Step-by-step guide to shopping with AI assistants

- Tips for staying safe while shopping online (secure payments, recognizing scams)

11. **AI for Travel: Navigating, Planning, and Booking**
    - How AI can help plan trips and navigate (Google Maps, travel booking apps)
    - Step-by-step guide to using AI for booking tickets, finding routes, etc.
    - Tips for using AI safely while traveling

12. **AI in Financial Management: Budgeting and Investment**
    - Introduction to AI tools for financial management (budgeting apps, investment advice)
    - Step-by-step guide to setting up and using financial apps
    - Tips on monitoring spending, investments, and financial security with AI

13. **Learning New Skills with AI: Language Learning, Hobbies, and More**
    - Overview of AI-powered learning apps (Duolingo, YouTube tutorials)
    - Step-by-step instructions to set up and use learning apps
    - Ideas for exploring new hobbies using AI

14. **Staying Informed: News, Weather, and Updates with AI**
    - How AI curates personalized news feeds (Google News, Apple News)
    - Step-by-step guide to setting up news alerts and updates
    - Using AI to get weather forecasts and local updates

15. **AI for Personal Safety: Emergency Assistance and Alerts**
    - Overview of AI apps that provide emergency alerts (Life360, medical alert apps)
    - Step-by-step guide to setting up emergency

contacts and alerts
- o Tips for using AI to stay safe

16. **Security and Privacy: Protecting Yourself in the AI World**
     - o Basic steps to protect privacy when using AI (passwords, data permissions)
     - o Understanding what data AI collects and how to manage it
     - o Tips for staying secure online

17. **Common Troubleshooting Tips for AI Devices**
     - o Simple solutions to common AI problems (voice assistant not responding, app crashes)
     - o Step-by-step guide to troubleshooting device settings
     - o Resources for further help (online forums, customer support)

18. **The Future of AI: What's Next?**
     - o A look at upcoming AI technologies and trends
     - o How AI might evolve and become more integrated into daily life
     - o Encouragement to continue learning and adapting

19. **FAQs: Common Questions from 60+ Users About AI**
     - o Frequently asked questions with simple answers
     - o Practical advice for overcoming common concerns and challenges
     - o Encouragement to keep exploring AI's potential

20. **Conclusion and Encouragement to Keep Exploring AI**
     - o Recap of key points from the eBook
     - o Encouragement to embrace AI and keep experimenting
     - o Resources for further learning and support

AI for Beginners: A Step-by-Step Guide for the 60+ Crowd

1. Introduction to AI (Artificial Intelligence)

What is AI?

Artificial Intelligence (AI) refers to computer systems that can perform tasks traditionally requiring human intelligence. It enables machines to understand natural language, process images, and make complex decisions by learning and adapting to new data over time. AI often involves advanced algorithms, machine learning, and neural networks that allow systems to improve based on experience, like how humans learn. In simple terms, AI can be thought of as a digital helper that becomes smarter and more capable as it gathers more information.

How AI Impacts Daily Life:

AI has seamlessly integrated into our daily routines, making many tasks more convenient, efficient, and personalized. Here are a few examples:

Smartphones: AI powers many features on our smartphones, like voice-activated assistants (such as Siri or Google Assistant), which allow users to set reminders, dictate messages, or ask for directions hands-free. Camera AI can adjust settings automatically, enhancing photo quality by recognizing lighting, faces, or specific scenes.

Smart Home Devices: Through devices like Amazon Alexa or Google Home, AI lets you control your lights, thermostat, or security cameras with simple voice commands. These devices can learn preferences over time, automatically adjusting your environment for comfort or efficiency, such as lowering the lights at a specific time or adjusting the thermostat based on the weather.

Healthcare: AI assists in managing medications, monitoring vital health statistics, and even predicting health issues before they become critical. For instance, wearable devices, such as smartwatches, use AI to monitor heart rate, detect irregularities, and send alerts for any abnormalities, helping with early detection and preventive care.

Online Shopping and Recommendations: E-commerce platforms use AI to offer personalized recommendations based on past purchases, preferences, and browsing history. AI can also assist with customer service through chatbots, providing answers to frequently asked questions or helping with returns or other inquiries.

Benefits of AI for Seniors:

AI offers numerous benefits for seniors, enhancing their independence, safety, and quality of life:

Simplifies Tasks: AI makes it easier and faster to perform everyday tasks. Voice-activated devices allow seniors to control various appliances, lights, or locks in their homes without needing to physically interact with them. Reminders for tasks such as taking medications or scheduling appointments help seniors stay organized and safe.

Health Management Support: Through wearable devices and smart health apps, seniors can monitor their blood pressure, heart rate, and even oxygen levels, all of which can be shared with caregivers or family members. Some AI programs can also send reminders for medications and health check-ups, reducing the risk of missed doses or forgotten appointments.

Keeps Seniors Connected: AI can make staying in touch with family and friends more accessible. Devices with voice and video call capabilities, such as smartphones or smart displays, make it easy for seniors to connect with loved ones, even if they are far away. Social apps and virtual communities powered by AI can also help seniors engage in meaningful interactions, participate in online classes, and explore hobbies.

Overall, AI is transforming how we interact with technology by making it more accessible and intuitive, especially for seniors who benefit from enhanced connectivity, personalized health support, and increased independence in managing daily routines. As AI continues to evolve, it has the potential to further enrich the lives of people across all age groups, fostering a world where technology intuitively meets the needs of its users.

2. Understanding Basic AI Terms and Concepts

Understanding some basic AI terms can make the concept of artificial intelligence more accessible. Here's a breakdown of commonly used AI terms and what they mean in straightforward language:

Machine Learning (ML): Machine learning is a type of AI that gives computers the ability to learn from data and experience without being explicitly programmed for every task. Think of it as training a computer to make predictions or decisions based on past information. For example, when you watch shows on a streaming platform like Netflix, machine learning algorithms analyze what you like and recommend similar shows or movies, adapting their suggestions as you watch more content.

Chatbots: Chatbots are AI programs designed to simulate conversation with users, often used in customer service. They can answer questions, provide assistance, and help guide users to the information they need, often right on a company's website. Chatbots range from simple systems that respond to basic questions to more advanced bots that use natural language processing (NLP) to understand and respond conversationally, giving the impression of chatting with a real person.

Virtual Assistants: Virtual assistants are advanced AI programs that help users complete tasks through voice commands. Examples include Siri (Apple), Alexa (Amazon), and Google Assistant. These assistants can do everything from answering questions and setting reminders to controlling smart home devices and navigating your day-to-day schedule. They improve over time, learning your preferences and adapting to your needs, making it easier to interact with technology through natural, spoken language.

Real-Life Examples of AI in Action:

AI has already become a helpful companion in everyday life, often so seamlessly integrated that it feels like second nature. Here are a few common examples of AI-powered assistants and tools:

Google Assistant: Google Assistant, available on most Android devices and as an app for iPhones, is a powerful tool that can perform a range of tasks. It can help you find information on the web, set reminders, give weather updates, check your calendar, and even control compatible smart home devices. By learning your routine, Google Assistant can offer personalized suggestions, such as traffic updates for your commute or reminding you to buy milk when you're near the grocery store.

Siri: Siri is Apple's voice-activated assistant, available on iPhones, iPads, and other Apple devices. Siri responds to questions, sets alarms, sends messages, plays music, and even makes recommendations based on your usage patterns. For instance, Siri might suggest a time to leave for an appointment based on current traffic. With Siri, iPhone users can perform various tasks hands-free, adding convenience and enhancing accessibility.

Alexa: Amazon's Alexa is a virtual assistant used with Amazon Echo devices and other smart speakers. It can control smart home appliances, like lights, thermostats, and locks, and can play music, provide news updates, or order products from Amazon. Alexa can also answer questions, read audiobooks, and provide entertainment with games or stories. For homes with multiple connected devices, Alexa acts as a central controller, making it simple to manage everything through voice commands.

These examples illustrate how AI has become an integral part of daily life, offering convenience, enhancing productivity, and making it easier to manage tasks. With each interaction, these AI systems continue to learn and improve, providing a more personalized and intuitive experience for users.

3. Getting Started with AI: Devices and Applications

AI is increasingly embedded in various devices we use daily, making our lives more efficient and personalized. Here's a look at some common devices that incorporate AI and how it enhances their functionality:

Smartphones (iPhone, Android): AI has transformed smartphones into powerful tools that go beyond basic communication. Through built-in AI-powered virtual assistants like Siri (iPhone) and Google Assistant (Android), users can manage daily tasks, set reminders, make calls, send messages, and even control smart home devices with voice commands. AI also powers features like facial recognition, predictive text, real-time language translation, and photo optimization by adjusting color, brightness, and sharpness to improve image quality automatically.

Tablets (iPad, Samsung): Tablets like the iPad and Samsung Galaxy Tab series leverage AI to boost productivity and convenience. Similar to smartphones, they come equipped with AI assistants (Siri on iPad, Google Assistant on Samsung tablets) that help users accomplish tasks quickly. These devices use AI to enhance graphics for smoother gaming, facilitate multitasking, and even optimize battery life based on usage patterns. They also offer advanced handwriting recognition and can convert handwritten notes to text, making them excellent for students and professionals.

Smart Speakers (Amazon Echo, Google Home): Smart speakers are voice-activated devices powered by virtual assistants like Amazon Alexa and Google Assistant. They can control various compatible smart home devices (lights, thermostats, locks), play music, set reminders, answer questions, and even shop online. They learn user preferences over time, making interactions more personalized. For example, if you ask Alexa for the daily news, it may provide updates from your favorite news sources and play a weather report based on your location.

How to Check if Your Device Supports AI:

You may already have AI capabilities on your device and not realize it. Here are some easy steps to confirm if your device has AI support:

Check for Voice Assistant Options: Go to your device's settings and look for options related to voice assistants. This might include "Siri & Search" for iPhones, "Google Assistant" settings on Android devices, or settings labeled "Alexa" on Amazon Echo-compatible devices.

Look for AI-Powered Apps: Common AI-driven apps like Siri, Google Assistant, or Alexa are typically pre-installed on devices with AI capabilities. If they're missing, you can download them from the app store, and setup is usually straightforward.

Setting Up AI on Your Devices:

Setting up AI features on your devices typically involves enabling a virtual assistant and following a few simple steps. Here's a quick guide for common devices:

1. Smartphone Setup

For iPhone:

- Go to Settings > Siri & Search.
- Toggle on Listen for "Hey Siri" and Press Side Button for Siri if they're not already enabled.
- Follow any prompts to customize Siri's responses, voice, or

accent.

For Android:

- Open the Google Assistant app or go to Settings > Google > Settings for Google Apps > Search, Assistant & Voice.
- Select Google Assistant and follow the setup prompts, which may include recording your voice for personalized recognition and customizing the assistant's language or voice.

2. Smart Speaker Setup

Plug in the smart speaker and wait for the device to start up.
Connect to Wi-Fi: Follow instructions on the accompanying app (Amazon Alexa app for Echo or Google Home app for Google devices) to connect the speaker to your Wi-Fi network.
Sign In and Link Services: You may need to sign into your account, customize settings, and link compatible smart home devices for a personalized experience.

Customize Settings: Adjust settings like news preferences, commute information, and favorite playlists to personalize your interactions with the device.

Summary

Setting up AI on your devices is easy and enhances the convenience and efficiency of managing daily tasks, controlling smart devices, and staying organized. Once enabled, AI features can handle everything from reminders and hands-free calling to personalized suggestions, making them a valuable addition to your digital routine.

4. Voice Assistants: Your Personal AI Helpers

Voice assistants are AI-powered digital tools that respond to spoken commands, making it easy to perform tasks, get information, and control other devices without needing to type or navigate menus. Popular voice assistants include Siri (Apple), Google Assistant (Google), and Alexa (Amazon). They can perform various functions, such as answering questions, setting reminders, playing music, and controlling compatible smart home devices. By simply speaking a command, users can access a range of services and features, making interactions with technology smoother, faster, and often hands-free.

Voice assistants are continuously improving through machine learning, which allows them to understand context, respond more accurately to natural language, and remember user preferences. As a result, they adapt to the user's style and habits, offering more personalized responses and recommendations over time.

How to Set Up a Voice Assistant

Setting up a voice assistant on your device is typically straightforward and only requires a few steps. Here's how to set up three of the most popular voice assistants:

1. Google Assistant (Android)
Google Assistant is integrated into most Android devices and is also available as an app for iOS.
Step 1: Open the Google app on your Android device.
Step 2: Tap on your profile picture or initial in the top right corner to open your account settings.
Step 3: Go to Assistant settings > Voice Match.
Step 4: Follow the prompts to enable Voice Match, which allows Google Assistant to recognize your voice specifically. You may also set up "Hey Google" or "OK Google" detection to activate it hands-

free.

After setup, try commands like "OK Google, what's on my calendar today?" or "Hey Google, play my favorite playlist."

2. Siri (iPhone)

Siri is Apple's built-in voice assistant for iOS devices like the iPhone and iPad.

Step 1: Go to Settings on your iPhone.

Step 2: Scroll to Siri & Search and tap on it.

Step 3: Toggle on Listen for 'Hey Siri' to enable hands-free activation. You can also enable Press Side Button for Siri to access Siri with a button press.

Step 4: Follow the on-screen prompts to train Siri to recognize your voice.

Once Siri is set up, you can try commands like "Hey Siri, remind me to pick up groceries at 5 PM" or "Hey Siri, show me nearby coffee shops."

3. Alexa (Amazon Echo)

Alexa is Amazon's voice assistant, primarily used with Echo devices but also available on mobile devices through the Alexa app.

Step 1: Download and open the Amazon Alexa app on your smartphone (available on iOS and Android).

Step 2: Sign in using your Amazon account.

Step 3: Follow the prompts to connect your Alexa-compatible device, such as an Amazon Echo, to Wi-Fi.

Step 4: Customize settings for news, skills, and smart home device integration within the app.

After setup, activate Alexa by saying "Alexa" followed by a command, like "Alexa, set an alarm for 7 AM" or "Alexa, dim the living room lights."

Common Commands for Voice Assistants

Here are some popular commands for each voice assistant that showcase their capabilities:

"Hey Siri, what's the weather today?"
Siri can give you real-time weather updates, forecasts, and alerts for your location or any specified area.

"OK Google, set a timer for 10 minutes."
Google Assistant can set timers for various tasks, making it handy for cooking, workouts, or time-sensitive reminders.

"Alexa, play some relaxing music."
Alexa can access various music streaming services like Amazon Music, Spotify, or Pandora to play your favorite tunes or a specific genre for different moods.

Summary of Voice Assistant Benefits

Voice assistants make everyday tasks simpler by allowing users to access information, set reminders, and manage smart devices through natural language. As they adapt to individual preferences, voice assistants become increasingly intuitive, providing users with a more personalized, convenient, and hands-free experience with their devices.

5. Using AI for Communication

AI has revolutionized the way we communicate, making it easier, faster, and more inclusive. Here are a few ways AI-driven tools enhance our ability to connect with others, bridging gaps in language, accessibility, and convenience.

1. Voice Typing

Voice typing allows you to speak directly into your phone or computer, and the device automatically converts your speech into text. This is particularly helpful when you're on the go, have limited mobility, or prefer hands-free operation. Voice typing is available on most smartphones and works seamlessly with texting, email, and even note-taking apps. Here's how to activate it on popular devices:

iPhone: Open the app where you want to type (like Messages or Notes), tap the microphone icon on the keyboard, and start speaking. Your words will appear as text on the screen.

Android: Open a text field, tap the microphone icon on the Google Keyboard (Gboard), and start talking. The speech-to-text feature will transcribe your words instantly.

With regular use, AI learns your voice and speech patterns, improving accuracy over time and allowing for faster, more natural communication without typing.

2. Language Translation

AI-powered translation tools have broken down language barriers, making it easier to communicate with people who speak different languages. Apps like Google Translate can instantly translate both written and spoken language. Here's how they work:

Text Translation: Type or paste text into Google Translate, select the source and target languages, and the app will translate it instantly. You can also scan text from images or documents using your phone's camera.

Voice Translation: Speak directly into Google Translate, and it will translate your spoken words into another language, displaying or reading aloud the translation. This is useful for live conversations and travel, as the app can serve as a personal interpreter in real-time. Other translation apps like Microsoft Translator and iTranslate offer similar features, with some allowing live conversation translation where two people speak in different languages and the app translates each person's words into the other's language, facilitating a more natural dialogue.

Using AI for Video Calls

Video calling platforms that use AI features make virtual meetings more convenient, accessible, and engaging. These platforms often incorporate AI-based noise suppression, background blurring, and automatic video adjustments for optimal call quality. Here's how to start a video call on popular apps:

1. Zoom

Zoom is widely used for personal and professional video calls. Here's how to set it up:

Step 1: Download the Zoom app from the App Store (iOS) or Google Play Store (Android), or access it through a web browser on your computer.
Step 2: Sign up for a free account or log in if you already have one.
Step 3: To start a call, open the app and tap on New Meeting. You can invite others by sharing the meeting ID or link.
Step 4: Zoom offers AI features like background blur and noise cancellation to improve call quality.

2. Google Meet
Google Meet is another popular video calling platform, especially convenient for users with a Google account:

Step 1: Open the Google Meet app on your phone or go to meet.google.com on your computer.
Step 2: Sign in with your Google account.
Step 3: Tap New Meeting to start a call. Share the link generated by Google Meet with participants to invite them.
Step 4: Google Meet includes AI-powered features like real-time captions and background noise suppression, making it easier for all participants to focus on the conversation.
Both Zoom and Google Meet leverage AI to provide a smoother, more immersive experience, particularly useful for those working remotely or maintaining long-distance connections.

Chatbots for Customer Service

Chatbots are AI-driven tools that simulate conversation and provide instant assistance on many websites and apps. Here's how they enhance the customer experience:

Instant Assistance: When you visit a website, you might see a chat window pop up asking if you need help. These chatbots are designed to answer frequently asked questions, guide you to relevant information, and even help with basic troubleshooting.

Ease of Use: Simply type your question or describe your issue, and the chatbot will provide answers based on its programming and knowledge base. Some chatbots are equipped with machine learning, enabling them to learn from previous interactions and provide more accurate responses over time.
Escalation to Human Support: If the chatbot can't answer your question, it typically offers to connect you with a human

representative for further assistance, ensuring that you get the help you need.

Summary of AI's Role in Communication

AI-powered tools have made communication faster, easier, and more accessible across languages, devices, and locations. Whether through voice typing, real-time translation, video calling enhancements, or chatbot assistance, AI enables people to connect in ways that were previously challenging, opening up new possibilities for personal and professional interactions around the world.

6. Staying Organized with AI: Calendars, Reminders, and More

AI tools and features can greatly simplify staying organized by helping you manage reminders, appointments, and daily routines. With voice commands, intelligent scheduling, and personalized prompts, AI ensures you won't miss important tasks, meetings, or personal routines. Here's how you can leverage AI to manage your schedule effectively:

1. Set Reminders

Setting reminders using voice assistants like Siri, Google Assistant, or Alexa allows you to quickly set up notifications for specific tasks. This is particularly helpful for remembering important daily or weekly tasks, such as taking medication, attending meetings, or completing household chores.

Example: "Hey Siri, remind me to take my medicine at 8 PM."

Other Scenarios: Reminders can be set for any time-sensitive task, like watering plants, making calls, or checking emails. For recurring tasks, you can specify the frequency ("Remind me every Monday at 10 AM to submit my weekly report").

Customizable: You can even set location-based reminders. For example, "Remind me to buy groceries when I'm near the supermarket."

These reminders are helpful for both one-time events and daily habits, ensuring that important tasks are completed on time.

2. Manage Calendars

AI-powered calendar apps, like Google Calendar and Apple Calendar, help you organize and streamline your appointments, meetings, and events. These calendars can sync across devices and apps, send reminders, and even suggest available times for events, making scheduling much easier.

Google Calendar: This app is compatible with most devices and integrates seamlessly with other Google apps (such as Gmail, where it can detect event invitations and automatically add them to your calendar). It also offers AI-based suggestions for setting up new events based on your location, availability, and preferences.

Apple Calendar: Apple's native calendar app is integrated with Siri, allowing you to add events, set reminders, and invite contacts with simple voice commands. It can also suggest event times based on your existing schedule and notify you of potential conflicts.

These AI-enhanced calendars not only help manage daily schedules but can also provide an overview of your week or month, making it easy to prioritize tasks and avoid conflicts.

Using Note-Taking Apps:

Note-taking apps equipped with AI features make it easy to capture, organize, and search your notes anytime, whether for personal use or professional projects. Here's a closer look at popular options:

1. Google Keep

Google Keep is a simple, user-friendly app designed for quick note-taking and list-making. It's great for jotting down ideas, creating checklists, or setting reminders on the go.

Step 1: Open the Google Keep app and tap on Take a note.
Step 2: Type your notes directly or tap the microphone icon to use voice-to-text, letting Google Keep transcribe your spoken words into notes.

Step 3: You can color-code, label, or add images to notes for easier organization and visual appeal.

Google Keep's AI-powered search feature makes it easy to find notes by keyword or category, so you can quickly access past notes even if you have a large collection.

2. Evernote

Evernote is a comprehensive note-taking app that organizes information into notebooks, making it ideal for managing multiple projects, topics, or categories.

Step 1: Create notebooks for different categories, such as work projects, personal goals, or travel planning.

Step 2: Inside each notebook, you can add notes, lists, images, and voice memos. For example, you could create a "Groceries" notebook with lists of food items to buy or use a "Work Ideas" notebook to store brainstorming notes.

Step 3: Evernote's AI-powered search can identify words in handwritten notes and scanned documents, making it a powerful tool for organizing information quickly and accurately.

Evernote's intelligent note suggestions and search capabilities make it easy to retrieve information without needing to remember specific details, making it invaluable for keeping track of diverse information.

Integrate AI into Daily Routines

AI tools and apps can support healthy habits, help manage time efficiently, and keep you on track with personalized reminders and prompts. Here are some practical ways to integrate AI into your daily life:

Set Daily Reminders: Use voice assistants like Alexa or Siri to set reminders for personal routines.

For instance:

Exercise: "Alexa, remind me to go for a walk every day at 7 AM."
Medication: Set recurring reminders for medication, ensuring you stay on track with your health regimen.
Hydration: Apps like WaterMinder use AI to remind you to drink water throughout the day based on your activity level and goals.

Manage Tasks with Todoist: Todoist is a popular task management app that uses AI to help prioritize and organize your tasks effectively.

Task Suggestions: Todoist offers AI-powered "Smart Schedule," which suggests optimal times for tasks based on your previous patterns.
Project Organization: Create different projects, such as "Work," "Home," and "Personal Goals," and organize tasks within these categories. You can add due dates, set reminders, and even create recurring tasks to stay organized.

Goal Tracking: Todoist allows you to track your productivity with charts and graphs, helping you stay motivated and monitor progress on daily, weekly, or monthly goals.
Summary of AI's Role in Daily Scheduling

From reminders to task tracking, AI-powered tools simplify routine management, helping you balance work, health, and personal commitments with ease. By integrating voice assistants, smart calendars, and specialized apps into your day-to-day activities, you can stay organized, enhance productivity, and ensure that important tasks aren't overlooked, giving you more time and energy for what matters most.

7. Health and Fitness Tracking with AI

Health apps on smartphones have become powerful tools to help users monitor and improve their physical well-being. These apps track various aspects of health, such as physical activity, sleep patterns, and heart rate, and provide personalized insights that can assist in setting and achieving fitness goals. Let's explore two of the most popular health apps and how they can benefit users:

1. Apple Health (iPhone)

Apple Health is a comprehensive health app pre-installed on iPhones. It collects and displays health-related data from your phone and connected devices, like the Apple Watch, providing a detailed overview of your physical well-being. Here are some key features:

Steps and Activity: Apple Health tracks daily steps, distance walked, and calories burned, providing a complete picture of your daily physical activity.

Heart Rate Monitoring: When paired with an Apple Watch, Apple Health monitors your heart rate continuously, identifying resting, walking, and workout heart rates. This data can alert users to potential heart health issues by recognizing irregularities or unusually high or low readings.

Sleep Tracking: Apple Health records sleep patterns, duration, and quality when connected to compatible devices, helping users understand their sleep habits and identify areas for improvement.

Integration with Other Apps: Apple Health integrates with third-party health and fitness apps, so you can see a consolidated view of your nutrition, mindfulness, and exercise data in one place.

2. Google Fit (Android)

Google Fit is Google's health-tracking app, designed for Android users but also available for iOS. It provides insights into physical activity and encourages users to set and meet fitness goals through personalized recommendations.

Physical Activity Monitoring: Google Fit tracks daily steps, activity minutes, and "Heart Points" (a measure of heart health based on activity intensity), encouraging users to achieve the recommended 150 minutes of moderate exercise per week.

Fitness Goals and Recommendations: Google Fit helps users set goals for active minutes and Heart Points, providing reminders and suggestions for reaching those goals based on individual activity levels.

Sleep and Heart Rate Tracking: Like Apple Health, Google Fit can track sleep and heart rate when connected with compatible wearables, helping users monitor overall health trends.

Integration with Wear OS and Third-Party Apps: Google Fit connects with smartwatches running on Wear OS and other fitness apps, such as Strava and MyFitnessPal, allowing users to view consolidated health data from multiple sources.

Setting Up Health Apps
Setting up health apps on your phone is simple and allows you to begin tracking health metrics and setting fitness goals quickly. Here's how to set up Apple Health and Google Fit:

1. Apple Health (iPhone)

Step 1: Open the Health app on your iPhone. If it's your first time using it, follow the on-screen prompts for the initial setup.

Step 2: The app will guide you through customizing your health profile, including information such as age, weight, height, and any specific health concerns.

Step 3: Choose the types of data you'd like to track, such as activity, nutrition, sleep, and mindfulness, and enable permissions for Apple Health to collect this information from compatible apps and devices.

Step 4: Review your Dashboard settings to arrange metrics that matter most to you on the home screen, like daily steps or sleep quality, so you can easily monitor your progress.

Once set up, Apple Health will automatically track daily activities and display personalized insights based on your goals and health metrics.

2. Google Fit (Android)

Step 1: Download Google Fit from the Google Play Store (if it's not already on your device) and open the app.

Step 2: Sign in with your Google account. The app will ask for permissions to access activity data from your phone and compatible devices.

Step 3: Set up fitness goals, such as daily steps or Heart Points, based on your desired activity level and health objectives.

Step 4: Google Fit will prompt you to allow notifications for reminders and activity tracking, so you receive timely updates on your progress.

With Google Fit, you can start monitoring your daily activities immediately and receive suggestions based on your performance and goals.

AI for Medication Tracking:

For individuals managing medications, AI-driven apps can be invaluable in ensuring medication is taken on time and as prescribed. AI can simplify medication tracking and offer tailored health recommendations:

Medication Tracking with Medisafe

Medisafe is a popular medication management app that uses AI to assist users in following their medication schedules accurately and consistently.

Reminders: Medisafe sends reminders for each dose, helping users stay on track even with complex schedules. This feature is particularly helpful for those taking multiple medications with different instructions.

Refill Alerts: The app can notify you when a medication supply is running low, making it easier to stay ahead on refills.
Health Information and Tips: Medisafe provides relevant health insights and alerts for potential drug interactions, offering a safer experience for users managing various medications.

AI-Generated Exercise and Health Suggestions

Many health apps now offer exercise routines and health suggestions tailored to the user's health profile. These AI-driven suggestions consider individual goals, activity levels, and health conditions.

Customized Exercise Plans: Apps like Google Fit and Apple Health may suggest exercise goals based on current activity patterns, adjusting them over time as you progress or based on specific health conditions (e.g., low-impact exercises for joint health).
Personalized Health Tips: Some apps analyze sleep and activity data to offer tips, such as reminders to get more sleep, drink water regularly, or reduce sedentary time, helping users maintain a balanced approach to health.

Summary of AI's Role in Health Apps

Health apps powered by AI are valuable tools for tracking and improving physical well-being. From monitoring steps and heart rate to managing medication schedules and personalizing exercise recommendations, AI in health apps offers users a proactive approach to managing their health. These tools promote healthy habits, enhance adherence to medication routines, and ultimately support a more balanced and mindful lifestyle.

8. Entertainment: Music, Movies, and Books with AI

How AI Recommends Content

AI has transformed how we discover and enjoy entertainment by learning about our preferences and suggesting relevant content tailored to our tastes. Through machine learning algorithms, AI observes user behavior, such as viewing history, liked or disliked items, and even the genres or artists we spend the most time with. This information is then used to make personalized recommendations, whether it's movies, music, or books.

How AI Learns Preferences

AI algorithms on platforms like Netflix, Spotify, and Audible continuously analyze what content we engage with. They track:

- **Viewing and Listening Habits**: How often we watch certain genres, rewatch episodes, skip songs, or pause shows midway.
- **Interactions**: Any thumbs-up, thumbs-down, or star ratings help refine AI's understanding of what we like.
- **Content Preferences**: Genres, actors, artists, and authors we tend to enjoy, as well as content length, themes, or moods.

Using this information, AI models identify patterns and similarities across large libraries of content, allowing them to recommend movies, shows, playlists, or books we're likely to enjoy. For instance, if someone consistently watches sci-fi movies, Netflix's AI will prioritize recommending other sci-fi content or genres that are commonly liked by sci-fi fans, like fantasy or thriller.

Using Streaming Platforms with AI Recommendations

AI recommendations are deeply integrated into popular streaming platforms, making it easier than ever to find new content without searching manually. Here's how to get the most from AI-driven recommendations on platforms like Netflix and Spotify:

1. Netflix (Movies and TV Shows)

Netflix's recommendation engine is designed to provide personalized suggestions based on viewing history and engagement patterns.

- **Step 1**: Open the **Netflix** app and log into your account. The homepage will display recommended content based on your profile.
- **Step 2**: **Browse Recommendations**: Netflix presents various categories such as "Top Picks for You," "Because You Watched…," and "Trending Now." Each category is curated by AI based on your previous interactions.
- **Step 3**: **Tap to Watch**: Click on a title to start watching or save it to "My List" if you want to watch it later. Engaging with the recommendations—whether by watching, rating, or saving—improves the accuracy of future suggestions.
- **Personalize Further**: You can create different profiles within a Netflix account, allowing each user to receive unique recommendations based on their specific viewing habits.

Netflix's AI adapts over time. If you start watching more comedies, for example, you'll notice that it starts recommending more lighthearted shows and fewer dramas.

2. Spotify (Music and Podcasts)

Spotify uses AI to create personalized playlists and discover new music based on listening patterns, genres, and individual song choices.

- **Step 1**: Open the **Spotify** app and log in.
- **Step 2**: **Explore AI-Generated Playlists**: Spotify's "Discover Weekly" and "Release Radar" playlists are curated by AI based on your recent listening history and genres you enjoy. Daily Mix playlists combine familiar tracks with new recommendations within specific genres.
- **Step 3**: **Create Playlists**: By creating playlists or liking songs, Spotify learns more about your taste. This improves the relevance of the "Made For You" section, where Spotify offers playlists specifically tailored to your preferences.
- **Step 4**: **Browse New Recommendations**: Under "Home" and "Browse," Spotify suggests artists, albums, and genres you may not have heard before but align with your tastes.

Spotify's recommendations get better the more you use the platform. For example, if you consistently listen to mellow acoustic music, Spotify may introduce you to new, similar artists or playlists for relaxation or concentration.

Finding Audiobooks with AI Recommendations

AI-powered audiobook platforms like Audible and Google Play Books make it simple to find books that match your interests, with recommendations based on past purchases, listens, and browsing history.

- **Audible**: Audible provides personalized suggestions based on your listening history, genre preferences, and the audiobooks in your library. When you first sign up, Audible may ask about your favorite genres to tailor initial recommendations.

- o **Browse Recommendations**: Audible's home screen shows sections like "Recommended for You," "Top Picks," and "Because You Listened...". These suggestions are AI-curated based on your listening habits and genre preferences.
- o **Add Books to Your Wishlist**: Adding titles to your wish list or library helps Audible understand your preferences more accurately.
- **Google Play Books**: Google Play Books also uses AI to recommend e-books and audiobooks. The more you browse, sample, and purchase, the better Google's recommendations become.
  - o **Explore "For You" Section**: Google Play Books offers a "For You" section with personalized recommendations. The app may also suggest books related to what's popular in genres you frequently read.
  - o **Sample Audiobooks**: Google Play Books allows you to sample audiobooks before purchase, and your sampling choices influence future recommendations.

Summary of AI's Role in Content Recommendations

AI-based recommendation systems on platforms like Netflix, Spotify, Audible, and Google Play Books enhance our entertainment experience by curating content based on our preferences. They use advanced algorithms to learn individual tastes and behaviors, offering personalized suggestions for movies, music, podcasts, and books. As we continue to interact with these platforms, their AI systems refine their recommendations, helping us discover content we're likely to enjoy without the need for lengthy searching.

9. Devices: Making Life Easier with AI

Introduction to Smart Home Technology

Smart home technology uses internet-connected devices to automate and enhance various household functions, making everyday tasks simpler, more efficient, and often hands-free. With smart devices, you can control lighting, adjust the thermostat, lock doors, or even run appliances by simply using voice commands or a smartphone app. The integration of AI with smart home technology has allowed devices to learn user preferences and patterns, creating a more personalized, comfortable, and secure home environment.

Key Benefits of Smart Home Technology

- **Convenience**: Control devices from anywhere with an app or voice command, whether you're home or away.
- **Energy Efficiency**: Smart thermostats, lights, and plugs allow you to optimize energy usage by setting schedules and reducing waste.
- **Enhanced Security**: Smart locks, cameras, and sensors offer added protection by allowing real-time monitoring and alerts.
- **Comfort**: AI-driven devices learn your preferences, adjusting lighting, temperature, or entertainment automatically to suit your lifestyle.

Setting Up Smart Devices

Smart home devices are generally easy to set up and come with step-by-step instructions. Here's how to set up some of the most popular smart devices:

1. Smart Lights

Smart lighting systems, like Philips Hue or Wyze, allow you to control brightness, color, and scheduling from a smartphone app or via voice commands.

- **Step 1**: **Install the Smart Bulb**: Replace your regular light bulb with a smart bulb in the desired fixture.
- **Step 2**: **Download the App**: Most smart bulbs have a dedicated app (like the Philips Hue app) available on the App Store or Google Play.
- **Step 3**: **Connect to Wi-Fi**: Open the app and follow prompts to connect the bulb to your Wi-Fi network. Some systems may require a central hub, while others connect directly to your Wi-Fi.
- **Step 4**: **Set Up Voice Commands**: If you're using a compatible voice assistant (like Alexa, Google Assistant, or Siri), link the device through the app to enable voice control.

Once set up, you can control smart lights with voice commands like "Alexa, dim the living room lights to 50%," or schedule lights to turn on and off at specific times.

2. Smart Thermostat

Smart thermostats, like Nest or Ecobee, adjust the temperature automatically based on your schedule and preferences, helping save on energy costs.

- **Step 1**: **Install the Thermostat**: Follow the manufacturer's instructions for installation, which typically involves replacing your existing thermostat. Many smart thermostats come with straightforward installation guides, but professional installation is recommended if you're unfamiliar with thermostat wiring.

- **Step 2**: **Connect to Wi-Fi**: Once installed, download the thermostat's app and connect the device to your Wi-Fi network.
- **Step 3**: **Set Temperature Schedules**: Use the app to create schedules based on your routine (e.g., lowering the temperature at night or when you're away).
- **Step 4**: **Voice Control Integration**: If you're using a voice assistant, link the thermostat in the app to enable voice commands.

With a smart thermostat, you can simply say, "Hey Google, set the thermostat to 72 degrees," or let the thermostat automatically adjust based on your habits and preferences.

Examples of Simplifying Daily Tasks with Smart Home Technology

With smart home technology, routine household tasks become quicker and easier, allowing you to manage home functions hands-free. Here are some examples:

- **Control Lighting**: "Alexa, turn off the living room lights."
  By controlling lighting with voice commands, you can adjust brightness or turn lights on and off without needing to get up. This is especially useful in rooms with multiple light fixtures or for those with mobility issues.
- **Adjust Temperature**: "Hey Google, set the thermostat to 72 degrees."
  Smart thermostats can make your home more comfortable by letting you adjust the temperature instantly or setting it to adjust automatically based on room occupancy or outside weather conditions.
- **Lock and Unlock Doors**: "Siri, lock the front door."
  Smart locks can be controlled from your phone or with voice commands, allowing you to lock doors remotely or let guests in without needing to be there in person.

- **Control Appliances**: "Alexa, start the coffee maker." Smart plugs can turn regular appliances like coffee makers, fans, or space heaters into smart devices, allowing you to control them remotely or set schedules so they're ready when you are.

Summary of Smart Home Technology

Smart home technology brings convenience, security, and efficiency into daily life by allowing users to control lights, thermostats, locks, and appliances with simple voice commands or smartphone apps. From adjusting the temperature to locking doors remotely, smart devices create a more comfortable and personalized living environment. With easy setup and compatibility with AI-powered voice assistants like Alexa, Google Assistant, and Siri, smart homes are increasingly accessible and beneficial for various lifestyle needs, enhancing convenience and efficiency at home.

10. Shopping Online Safely with AI

Using AI for Online Shopping

AI has revolutionized the online shopping experience by making it faster, more personalized, and convenient. From helping find specific products to comparing prices and even placing orders, AI assistants like Amazon Alexa and Google Assistant simplify and enhance the shopping process. Through machine learning, AI learns user preferences and habits, enabling smarter recommendations and easier shopping with voice commands.

How AI Enhances Online Shopping

AI in online shopping platforms allows for:

- **Personalized Recommendations**: AI learns from your shopping history and browsing patterns to suggest items based on your tastes, often displaying related or complementary products to enhance your experience.
- **Efficient Price Comparison**: AI-powered tools quickly compare prices across websites, helping you find the best deals without having to search manually.
- **Seamless Reordering and List Management**: Voice assistants enable easy reordering of frequent purchases and allow users to create shopping lists hands-free, streamlining the entire process.

Shopping with Voice Assistants

Voice assistants like Alexa and Google Assistant have made online shopping as easy as speaking a command. Here's how to use them effectively:

1. Amazon Alexa (for Shopping on Amazon)

Alexa, Amazon's AI-powered voice assistant, is designed to simplify shopping, especially for products available on Amazon. You can place orders, add items to a shopping list, and track packages hands-free.

- **Adding Items to a Shopping List**: Say, "Alexa, add batteries to my shopping list," and Alexa will add the item to your list in the Alexa app, where you can review and purchase it later.
- **Reordering**: If you frequently order certain items, Alexa can make reordering easy. You can say, "Alexa, reorder paper towels," and Alexa will place the order based on your previous purchase history.
- **Direct Purchasing**: For Prime members, Alexa can help place orders directly. Say, "Alexa, order [product]," and Alexa will confirm and purchase the item for you, saving time and effort.
- **Deals and Discounts**: Alexa can notify you about exclusive deals and suggest discounts on frequently purchased items, making it easier to save on regular purchases.

2. Google Shopping (for Product Search and Comparison)

Google Shopping integrates with Google Assistant and the Google app to allow users to search for products, compare prices, and even purchase items from a variety of online stores.

- **Product Search**: Open the Google app and type or voice-search for the product you're interested in (e.g., "best wireless earbuds"). Google Shopping will display a list of available options, prices, and retailers.

- **Price Comparison**: Google Shopping provides a side-by-side comparison of products across different sellers, showing the best prices and delivery options. This feature is especially useful for comparing prices without visiting multiple websites.
- **Voice-Activated Shopping**: You can use Google Assistant to add items to your shopping list with commands like, "Hey Google, add milk to my shopping list." Google Assistant can then provide product suggestions based on previous purchases and local availability.

Safety Tips for Online Shopping

While AI makes online shopping easier, it's essential to follow safety practices to protect your personal information and avoid scams. Here are some key safety tips:

- **Use Secure Payment Methods**: Always opt for secure payment methods, such as credit cards or PayPal, which offer buyer protection in case of fraudulent transactions. Avoid using debit cards, as they provide less security for online purchases.
- **Shop on Trusted Websites**: Stick to well-known retailers and check that the website's URL begins with "https://" (the "s" stands for secure). Look for security certificates, like a padlock icon near the URL bar, which indicates a site's secure connection.
- **Beware of Suspicious Links and Offers**: Avoid clicking on links from unsolicited emails, texts, or ads that promise deals that seem too good to be true. Scammers often use these tactics to collect personal information or steal credit card details.
- **Enable Two-Factor Authentication**: For extra protection, enable two-factor authentication (2FA) on your shopping accounts. This adds a layer of security by requiring a code sent to your phone or email before logging in.

- **Check Purchase Confirmations and Statements**: Regularly monitor your email for order confirmations and check bank statements for unauthorized transactions. Reporting suspicious activity immediately can prevent potential fraud.

Summary of AI's Role in Online Shopping

AI-driven tools and voice assistants like Alexa and Google Assistant enhance online shopping by providing personalized recommendations, quick price comparisons, and convenient list management. Voice-activated commands make shopping even easier, especially for frequently purchased items or reordering essentials. By following safety tips and using secure payment methods, shoppers can enjoy the convenience of AI-powered shopping while protecting personal information.

11. AI for Travel: Navigating, Planning, and Booking

AI-Assisted Travel Planning

AI is transforming the way we plan, book, and enjoy travel experiences, making the process smoother, more personalized, and efficient. With AI-driven tools and apps, travelers can find routes, receive real-time updates, explore local attractions, and even book flights and accommodations. These tools also offer personalized recommendations based on user preferences, helping travelers make the most of their journeys with minimal hassle.

How AI Enhances Travel Planning

AI simplifies travel planning in several ways:

- **Real-Time Navigation and Traffic Updates**: AI-driven navigation tools like Google Maps provide real-time information on traffic, estimated arrival times, and alternative routes to avoid delays.
- **Personalized Recommendations**: AI analyzes your preferences and search history to recommend restaurants, attractions, and activities that align with your interests.
- **Efficient Booking**: AI-powered platforms like Google Flights and Airbnb make it easy to find flights and accommodations that match your budget and preferences, saving time and money.

Using Google Maps for Travel Planning

Google Maps is an essential AI-powered tool for travelers, offering not just directions but also insights on local places, estimated travel times, and real-time traffic updates.

- **Getting Directions**: Enter your destination in Google Maps, and the app will suggest multiple routes with estimated travel times. It also shows current traffic conditions and recommends the fastest route based on real-time data.
- **Estimated Travel Times**: Google Maps provides estimated arrival times based on traffic, distance, and average speeds. This feature helps travelers plan ahead and reach their destinations on time.
- **Local Recommendations**: Google Maps uses AI to suggest nearby restaurants, attractions, and popular landmarks based on your current location. The "Explore" feature provides suggestions tailored to your preferences, such as highly-rated coffee shops, museums, and scenic views.

By using Google Maps, travelers can enjoy a guided experience that adapts to their needs, making exploration easier and more enjoyable.

Booking Tickets with AI

AI-driven platforms for booking flights and accommodations streamline the reservation process by comparing prices, displaying reviews, and offering secure booking options. Here's a closer look at two popular AI-powered tools for travel bookings:

1. Google Flights (for Booking Flights)

Google Flights is an AI-powered platform designed to help users find the best flight deals based on their destination, dates, and budget. It provides flexible search options and real-time price tracking, helping travelers make informed choices.

- **Search for Flights**: Enter your origin, destination, and travel dates. Google Flights will display a list of available flights with various airlines and price ranges.
- **Compare Prices**: Google Flights compares prices from different airlines and provides insights on whether prices are

likely to go up or down. The "Price Graph" and "Date Grid" features allow travelers to see how prices vary across different dates, making it easier to choose budget-friendly options.

- **Book Directly**: Once you select a flight, Google Flights directs you to the airline's website or a travel agency to complete the booking securely. This integration helps ensure a seamless booking process without needing to navigate multiple websites.

Google Flights is especially helpful for travelers looking to book flights within a budget, as it provides alerts on fare changes and recommends optimal booking times for the best deals.

2. Airbnb (for Booking Accommodations)

Airbnb uses AI to personalize accommodation recommendations based on the traveler's preferences, previous bookings, and destination. It provides a wide variety of options, from budget-friendly stays to luxurious vacation homes.

- **Browse Accommodations**: Enter your destination, travel dates, and guest details to browse a range of accommodations, from private rooms to entire homes.
- **Check Reviews and Ratings**: AI-powered sorting and filtering options let you view properties based on ratings, amenities, and guest reviews, making it easy to find quality options that suit your needs.
- **Secure Booking**: Airbnb's secure booking system ensures that payments and reservations are processed safely. You can communicate with hosts directly within the app to confirm details and get personalized recommendations for your stay.

Airbnb's AI-driven recommendation engine makes it easier for travelers to find accommodations that match their needs, ensuring a comfortable and convenient stay.

Safety Tips for Using AI While Traveling

While AI tools greatly enhance travel convenience, it's essential to follow some safety guidelines to ensure a smooth experience and avoid potential issues.

- **Double-Check Booking Details**: Before confirming any bookings, review the details, including dates, times, and locations. For flights, ensure you understand airline policies on cancellations and changes.
- **Use Trusted Apps for Navigation**: Stick to well-known, reliable apps like Google Maps, Waze, or Apple Maps for navigation. Avoid downloading unfamiliar or unverified apps, especially when abroad.
- **Enable Location Sharing with Trusted Contacts**: For added safety, share your live location with trusted friends or family members, especially when exploring unfamiliar places.
- **Be Cautious with Free Wi-Fi**: Avoid accessing sensitive information or making transactions on public Wi-Fi networks. Use a Virtual Private Network (VPN) when connecting to public Wi-Fi to keep your data secure.

Summary of AI's Role in Travel Planning

AI-driven travel tools like Google Maps, Google Flights, and Airbnb simplify the entire travel planning process, from finding routes and local recommendations to booking flights and accommodations. With AI's ability to learn user preferences, travelers receive personalized suggestions that enhance their travel experience, making it easier to explore new destinations with confidence. By following safety guidelines and using trusted platforms, travelers can enjoy the convenience of AI while staying secure on their journey.

12. AI in Financial Management: Budgeting and Investment

AI Tools for Managing Finances

AI-powered financial tools are transforming personal finance by providing users with the ability to track spending, set budgets, manage investments, and gain insights into their financial health. These tools analyze spending patterns, track income and expenses, offer investment recommendations, and help set financial goals. By automating and simplifying these tasks, AI-based financial tools empower users to make smarter financial decisions and stay organized with minimal effort.

Key Benefits of AI in Personal Finance

- **Budgeting Assistance**: AI tools analyze spending habits and help create realistic budgets based on income and expenses.
- **Investment Insights**: AI-powered apps offer insights and recommendations based on market trends and your investment profile.
- **Goal Tracking**: Financial apps enable users to set and track goals, such as saving for a trip, emergency fund, or retirement.

Popular AI Tools for Financial Management

Here's a closer look at some of the most commonly used AI-powered financial tools:

1. Mint

Mint is a comprehensive personal finance app that helps users track spending, create budgets, and monitor their credit score. Mint's AI-powered analytics categorize spending and provide insights into areas where you may want to save or adjust spending.

- **Spending Tracking**: Mint connects to your bank accounts, credit cards, and loans, automatically tracking and categorizing each transaction. This enables users to see where their money goes each month.
- **Budget Creation**: Based on your spending habits, Mint helps you set up a budget that fits your financial lifestyle. The app also provides alerts when you approach budget limits in specific categories, helping you control spending.
- **Savings Goals**: Mint allows you to create custom savings goals (such as "Emergency Fund" or "Vacation") and track your progress, providing motivation and accountability.

2. Robinhood

Robinhood is an investment platform that uses AI to provide insights, news, and recommendations, making investing accessible to both beginners and seasoned investors. It allows users to buy and sell stocks, ETFs, cryptocurrencies, and more.

- **Investment Insights**: Robinhood's AI analyzes market data and trends to provide insights and recommendations that can help inform your investment decisions.
- **Real-Time Market News**: Robinhood delivers real-time updates and news relevant to your investments. Its AI also tailors news recommendations based on your portfolio and areas of interest.
- **Portfolio Tracking**: The app provides a snapshot of your portfolio's performance and breakdowns of investment types, making it easy to monitor gains, losses, and overall asset distribution.

Step-by-Step Guide to Financial Apps

Getting started with financial apps is simple, and these tools guide you through setting up budgets, tracking spending, and managing investments. Here's a quick guide on setting up two popular financial management apps:

1. Mint

Mint is ideal for budget-conscious users who want to monitor spending and stay on top of monthly budgets.

- **Step 1**: **Download the Mint App**: Get the app from the App Store (iOS) or Google Play (Android).
- **Step 2**: **Connect Your Bank Accounts**: After creating an account, securely link your bank, credit card, and loan accounts. Mint will automatically pull in transaction data and categorize expenses.
- **Step 3**: **Set Up a Budget**: Mint will analyze your spending patterns and suggest budget categories (like groceries, entertainment, and bills). You can set monthly limits for each category based on your financial goals.
- **Step 4**: **Review Spending and Adjust as Needed**: Use Mint's insights to see where you might need to adjust spending. Mint will send alerts when you approach or exceed your budget, helping you stay in control.

2. Personal Capital

Personal Capital is designed for those looking to manage both spending and investments, offering tools for tracking net worth, portfolio performance, and retirement planning.

- **Step 1**: **Download and Open the App**: Personal Capital is available on iOS, Android, and desktop.
- **Step 2**: **Link Financial Accounts**: Connect your bank accounts, credit cards, investment accounts, and retirement

accounts. The app will aggregate this information to provide a complete view of your finances.

- **Step 3**: **Explore Investment Tracking**: The app's AI analyzes your investment portfolio, offering insights on diversification, fees, and potential growth. Personal Capital also provides personalized financial advice.
- **Step 4**: **Set Financial Goals**: Use the app to set long-term goals, like retirement or a major purchase, and track your progress. Personal Capital's Retirement Planner provides detailed projections based on your current savings and spending patterns.

Security Tips for Using Financial Apps

Given the sensitive nature of financial data, it's essential to follow security best practices when using these apps. Here are some tips to ensure your information stays protected:

- **Use Strong Passwords**: Choose unique and complex passwords for each financial app. Avoid using easily guessed information (like birthdays or simple sequences) and change your passwords regularly.
- **Enable Two-Factor Authentication (2FA)**: Most financial apps offer two-factor authentication for added security. This requires a second form of verification (such as a code sent to your phone) when logging in, making it harder for unauthorized users to access your account.
- **Regularly Review Transactions**: Check your transactions for any unauthorized activity, especially if your financial app links directly to your bank accounts or credit cards. Report any suspicious activity immediately.
- **Log Out After Use**: If you're using a shared or public device, always log out after using financial apps to prevent unauthorized access.
- **Avoid Public Wi-Fi for Financial Transactions**: Public Wi-Fi networks are more vulnerable to hackers. If you need

to access financial apps while on the go, use a secure mobile network or VPN for an added layer of security.

Summary of AI's Role in Financial Management

AI-powered financial tools like Mint and Robinhood simplify budgeting, tracking, and investing by offering personalized insights, automated tracking, and intelligent recommendations. By following best practices for setup and security, users can take full advantage of these tools to stay organized, save effectively, and make informed financial decisions with greater confidence.

13. Learning New Skills with AI: Language Learning, Hobbies, and More

AI-Powered Learning Apps

AI-powered learning apps have transformed the way we acquire new skills and knowledge, making learning more accessible, engaging, and personalized. By leveraging AI, these apps can adapt to individual learning styles, track progress, and provide instant feedback, helping users master languages, develop professional skills, or explore creative hobbies. Here's a closer look at some popular AI-enhanced learning platforms and how to get started with them.

How AI Enhances Learning in Apps

AI-driven learning apps provide several key benefits:

- **Personalized Learning Paths**: AI assesses a user's skill level and adapts lessons to ensure optimal pacing and difficulty.
- **Instant Feedback**: Learners receive immediate feedback on exercises, helping them correct mistakes and reinforce learning.
- **Engagement and Motivation**: Many apps use gamification, like points, rewards, and streaks, to make learning fun and maintain user motivation.
- **Progress Tracking**: AI helps track progress over time, highlighting strengths and areas that need more focus, allowing users to achieve their learning goals more effectively.

Popular AI-Powered Learning Apps

Let's explore two popular AI-powered learning platforms and how they make learning interactive and enjoyable:

1. Duolingo (for Language Learning)

Duolingo is a popular language-learning app that uses AI to make language acquisition fun and accessible. The app adapts to your learning pace, creating a game-like experience with levels, streaks, and achievements to keep you motivated.

- **Interactive Exercises**: Duolingo offers a variety of activities, including translation, speaking, and listening exercises, designed to reinforce vocabulary, grammar, and pronunciation. The app uses AI to adjust the difficulty of exercises based on your performance, ensuring steady progress.
- **Gamified Learning**: Points, streaks, and rewards add a competitive element, motivating users to complete lessons regularly.
- **AI-Based Review Sessions**: Duolingo's AI identifies words and concepts that users struggle with and creates targeted review sessions to reinforce these areas, helping learners retain what they've learned.

2. MasterClass (for Learning from Experts)

MasterClass is an educational platform offering lessons from industry experts and celebrities, covering topics from cooking to filmmaking, business, and more. Each class features high-quality video lessons designed to provide a deep dive into each subject.

- **Expert-Led Classes**: MasterClass offers courses taught by experts like Gordon Ramsay, Serena Williams, and Stephen Curry, providing an insider's perspective on their fields.
- **High-Quality, Structured Lessons**: Classes are professionally filmed and organized into chapters with downloadable materials, allowing users to study in a structured and enjoyable way.
- **Flexible Learning**: Unlike gamified learning apps, MasterClass emphasizes flexibility, allowing users to learn at their own pace and focus on areas of interest. The platform also offers AI-based recommendations based on the user's progress and preferences, suggesting additional courses aligned with their learning journey.

Setting Up Learning Apps

Getting started with AI-powered learning apps is simple, and most platforms provide guided setups to personalize the experience. Here's a step-by-step guide for Duolingo and Skillshare:

1. Duolingo (for Language Learning)

- **Step 1**: **Download the App**: Install Duolingo from the App Store (iOS) or Google Play (Android).
- **Step 2**: **Choose a Language**: After setting up your profile, select the language you want to learn. Duolingo offers over 30 languages, from widely spoken ones like Spanish and French to lesser-known languages.
- **Step 3**: **Set Your Daily Goal**: Duolingo will ask you to set a daily goal for learning (e.g., 5, 10, or 15 minutes a day). The app will remind you to practice daily, helping you develop a consistent learning habit.
- **Step 4**: **Start Daily Lessons**: Begin with basic lessons, covering vocabulary, grammar, and pronunciation. Duolingo's AI adapts the lesson difficulty as you progress, making the experience both challenging and achievable.

2. Skillshare (for Creative and Professional Skills)

Skillshare is a platform offering thousands of courses in various fields, such as design, photography, business, and technology.

- **Step 1**: **Sign Up**: Create an account on the Skillshare website or app. Skillshare offers a free trial period, allowing new users to explore courses without commitment.
- **Step 2**: **Browse Courses**: Use the search feature to find courses in your area of interest, such as writing, photography, or marketing. Skillshare's AI suggests courses based on your activity, making it easier to discover content aligned with your learning goals.
- **Step 3**: **Learn at Your Own Pace**: Unlike structured lesson plans, Skillshare allows you to watch lessons and practice at your own speed. The app also offers community-driven projects and workshops for hands-on learning experiences.
- **Step 4**: **Track Your Progress**: Skillshare keeps track of completed lessons, helping you monitor progress and stay motivated.

Exploring New Hobbies

AI-powered tools make it easy to dive into new hobbies and interests. Many platforms offer step-by-step tutorials and guided sessions for creative hobbies, allowing you to start learning from scratch. Here are a few popular options for exploring hobbies:

- **YouTube for Tutorials**: YouTube offers free, high-quality tutorials for nearly any hobby you can imagine, from cooking and gardening to painting and photography. Many creators produce beginner-friendly content and offer AI-enhanced captions and translation, making learning accessible worldwide.
- **Udemy for Diverse Hobbies**: Udemy is an online learning platform with courses on various hobbies, from coding and

photography to baking and yoga. AI-powered recommendations make it easy to find courses suited to your level and interests.

- **Pinterest for DIY Inspiration**: Pinterest is a visual discovery platform ideal for finding ideas and inspiration for DIY projects, crafts, home improvement, and more. AI-powered suggestions help you discover projects and materials based on your interests.

Summary of AI's Role in Learning and Exploring New Hobbies

AI-powered learning apps like Duolingo and MasterClass offer tailored, engaging, and accessible ways to acquire new skills and expand knowledge. With features like gamification, expert-led lessons, and personalized recommendations, these platforms cater to a wide range of learners. By following simple setup instructions, users can dive into language learning, creative hobbies, or professional development at their own pace. Additionally, resources like YouTube, Udemy, and Pinterest provide further opportunities to explore new hobbies with step-by-step guidance, making AI-enhanced learning a versatile and enjoyable experience.

14. Staying Informed: News, Weather, and Updates with AI

How AI Curates Your News

AI-driven news platforms curate personalized news feeds, delivering stories and updates that align with your interests and reading habits. By analyzing your interactions, such as the types of articles you read, the topics you follow, and the amount of time spent on different categories, AI tailors news recommendations to make them more relevant. This customization ensures you see the stories that matter most, whether they're breaking news, business updates, sports, or technology trends.

Key Benefits of AI in News Curation

- **Personalized Content**: AI adapts your feed to highlight stories related to your interests, reducing the time you spend searching for relevant articles.
- **Breaking News Alerts**: AI identifies trending or urgent news and sends alerts in real-time so you stay informed.
- **Broader Discovery**: AI-powered apps also introduce you to related topics or sources that you may not have explored, broadening your news consumption while aligning with your interests.
- **Reduced Information Overload**: By prioritizing content that aligns with your preferences, AI helps avoid information overload, focusing on high-interest stories.

Setting Up News Alerts

Personalizing your news feed and setting up alerts is simple, and most popular news apps offer intuitive setups. Here's how to get started with Google News and Apple News, two popular AI-powered news platforms.

1. Google News

Google News uses AI to deliver a personalized experience by analyzing your reading preferences and engagement patterns. It provides a "For You" section that highlights top stories based on your interests and sends real-time alerts for breaking news.

- **Step 1**: **Download the Google News App**: Available for iOS and Android, the app provides access to news from various sources worldwide.
- **Step 2**: **Follow Topics of Interest**: After signing in, navigate to the "Following" tab and search for topics, sources, or keywords that interest you, such as "Technology," "Climate Change," or specific publications. You can follow as many topics as you want, and Google News will prioritize them in your feed.
- **Step 3**: **Get Daily Updates**: Enable notifications within the app to receive daily summaries and breaking news alerts. Google News AI curates a personalized "Daily Briefing" with key highlights that match your preferences, making it easy to stay up-to-date on topics that matter to you.

2. Apple News

Apple News also uses AI to curate content based on user preferences and offers a customized feed with top stories and breaking news. Available on iOS devices, Apple News provides access to various news sources, including premium content through Apple News+.

- **Step 1**: **Customize News Preferences**: Open the Apple News app and go to "Following." From here, you can select channels, topics, and categories that interest you, such as "World News," "Health," or specific publishers.

- **Step 2**: **Enable Notifications for Breaking News**: In the app settings, enable notifications for breaking news and trending stories to get real-time updates. You can choose which channels or topics to receive notifications from, ensuring you only get alerts relevant to your interests.
- **Step 3**: **Adjust the "Today" Feed**: Apple News allows you to personalize the "Today" feed by favoriting or hiding sources. AI learns from these interactions, tailoring the feed to your preferences over time.

By setting up personalized alerts on Google News and Apple News, you ensure you stay informed on your favorite topics without needing to sift through unrelated stories.

Getting Weather Updates

AI-powered weather apps offer accurate, real-time updates and forecasts, helping users stay informed about changing conditions. Here's how you can use voice assistants and weather apps for quick access to weather information:

- **Voice Assistants for Quick Updates**: Voice assistants like Google Assistant, Alexa, and Siri provide instant weather updates with simple commands. For example, saying, "Hey Google, what's the weather today?" gives you an immediate forecast for your current location, covering temperature, humidity, and weather conditions (like rain or sunshine).
- **Detailed Forecasts with Weather Apps**: For more in-depth information, apps like **AccuWeather**, **The Weather Channel**, and **Weather Underground** provide 24-hour forecasts, weekly outlooks, radar maps, and severe weather alerts.
  - **AccuWeather**: AccuWeather's AI-powered "MinuteCast" feature provides hyper-localized

forecasts by the minute, which are especially useful for planning activities around potential weather changes.

o **The Weather Channel**: With AI-enhanced radar maps and future-cast models, The Weather Channel provides visual data on precipitation, storm tracking, and more. Its alerts for severe weather conditions help users stay safe and prepared.

o **Weather Underground**: Known for its highly detailed data, Weather Underground provides hyper-local reports and AI-generated insights based on data from thousands of weather stations. This can be helpful for travelers or anyone needing precise, location-specific information.

Summary of AI's Role in News and Weather Updates

AI-powered apps like Google News, Apple News, and various weather platforms personalize and streamline information, making it easier to stay informed. With curated news alerts based on reading habits and real-time weather updates tailored to your location, AI tools save time and enhance relevance. These AI-enhanced resources make it possible to enjoy a customized experience with fewer interruptions, keeping you updated on the topics and conditions that matter most.

15. AI for Personal Safety: Emergency Assistance and Alerts

AI for Safety and Alerts

AI-driven safety apps are transforming how we manage personal safety and emergency preparedness, offering real-time location tracking, automated alerts, and quick access to emergency contacts. These apps, such as Life360 and various medical alert platforms, use AI to keep you connected with family and support networks, helping them monitor your location, receive alerts, and respond quickly in case of emergencies. AI in these tools provides an added layer of protection, whether you're keeping track of family members, managing a health condition, or preparing for unforeseen situations.

Key Benefits of AI for Safety

- **Real-Time Tracking**: AI allows for live location tracking, so family members can monitor each other's whereabouts, ensuring everyone's safety.
- **Automated Alerts**: Apps can automatically send notifications to emergency contacts when an unusual event occurs, like arriving late or entering a designated danger zone.
- **Health and Medical Alerts**: Medical alert apps use AI to monitor health conditions and alert caregivers or family members in case of a health emergency.
- **Quick Access to Help**: AI-powered emergency setups allow users to reach their contacts and emergency services instantly.

Setting Up Emergency Alerts

Using safety apps with AI capabilities is a straightforward way to enhance your preparedness and keep loved ones informed about your safety. Here's a guide to setting up two commonly used apps: Life360 for family tracking and medical alert apps for health management.

1. Life360 (Family Safety and Location Tracking)

Life360 is a family safety app that offers real-time location sharing, geofencing alerts, and crash detection, allowing family members to keep track of each other and receive alerts if someone needs help.

- **Step 1**: **Download the Life360 App**: Available on iOS and Android, Life360 is free to download, with additional paid features for premium tracking and alert options.
- **Step 2**: **Set Up Your Profile**: After creating an account, add personal information to customize your profile. You can then invite family members to join your "Circle," allowing them to view your location and receive alerts.
- **Step 3**: **Add Emergency Contacts and Locations**: Designate specific emergency contacts who will receive alerts. Set up geofenced locations (such as "Home" or "School") so Life360 can send automatic notifications when you enter or leave these areas.
- **Step 4**: **Enable Safety Features**: Life360 includes features like "Crash Detection" and "SOS" mode. When enabled, these settings alert family members if the app detects an unexpected incident, such as a car accident. Users can also trigger an SOS alert manually to notify their Circle of an emergency.

Life360's AI analyzes location and movement data to enhance safety, making it particularly useful for families with teenagers, seniors, or those with medical needs.

2. Medical Alert Apps (for Health and Emergency Situations)

Medical alert apps, such as Medical ID or Red Panic Button, provide users with emergency response options tailored to their health needs. These apps can be invaluable for individuals with medical conditions who may need quick access to emergency contacts or health information.

- **Step 1**: **Install the App**: Choose a medical alert app that suits your needs, such as Medical ID (for sharing health info with first responders) or Red Panic Button (for quick alerts to emergency contacts).
- **Step 2**: **Enter Health Information**: In Medical ID, you can input important health information, such as allergies, blood type, medical conditions, and medications. This information can be accessed by emergency responders if necessary.
- **Step 3**: **Set Up Alerts and Emergency Contacts**: Designate emergency contacts who will receive notifications if you activate an alert. Some apps offer customizable alert options, like sending your real-time location to contacts when an alert is triggered.
- **Step 4**: **Enable Quick Access**: Many medical alert apps integrate with your phone's lock screen, allowing you to access the app or send alerts quickly without unlocking the device. Some apps can be triggered by a specific button press or shortcut for rapid access in emergencies.

Medical alert apps are particularly useful for individuals with health concerns or disabilities, as they can help ensure that medical information and emergency contacts are readily available.

Using AI to Stay Safe: Smartphone Emergency Settings

Your smartphone likely includes built-in emergency settings, and AI enhances these features by enabling faster communication and coordination with emergency contacts. Setting up emergency contacts in your smartphone is a key safety feature:

- **Set Up Emergency Contacts**: In your smartphone's settings, designate emergency contacts who can be reached easily. On iPhone, go to **Health** > **Medical ID** to add emergency contacts, which first responders can access directly from the lock screen. For Android, go to **Settings** > **Safety & Emergency** > **Emergency Contacts** to add names and numbers for quick access.
- **Use the Emergency SOS Feature**: Both iOS and Android devices have an SOS feature that can call emergency services and notify emergency contacts with your location:
  - **On iPhone**: Press and hold the side button along with either volume button to activate SOS. The phone will automatically call emergency services and notify your designated contacts.
  - **On Android**: Press the power button five times to activate Emergency SOS. It will call emergency services and send location details to your chosen contacts if enabled in settings.

These emergency settings are crucial as they allow you to quickly connect with help in an urgent situation, whether it's a medical emergency, accident, or safety threat.

Summary of AI's Role in Safety and Alerts

AI-powered safety apps, like Life360 and medical alert platforms, enhance personal safety by providing real-time location tracking, automated emergency alerts, and health monitoring. Through Life360's family tracking or medical alert systems for health emergencies, AI simplifies the process of staying connected and prepared. Built-in smartphone emergency settings further ensure quick access to help, adding another layer of security. By setting up emergency contacts, enabling alerts, and familiarizing yourself with these tools, you can use AI to stay safe and ensure loved ones are informed and prepared to respond in case of an emergency.

16. Security and Privacy: Protecting Yourself in the AI World

Basic Security Steps

In today's digital age, securing your online accounts and personal information is crucial. Following basic security steps can significantly reduce the risk of unauthorized access, data breaches, and identity theft. By using strong passwords, enabling two-factor authentication, managing app permissions, and practicing caution online, you can protect your data and maintain privacy.

Key Security Practices

- **Use Strong, Unique Passwords**: Creating unique, complex passwords for each of your accounts is essential for safeguarding against hackers. A strong password typically includes:
  o **Length**: At least 12 characters.
  o **Character Variety**: A mix of upper and lowercase letters, numbers, and special characters.
  o **Avoid Personal Information**: Avoid using easily guessed information, like birthdays, names, or common phrases.

  Use a **password manager** (like LastPass, Bitwarden, or 1Password) to generate and store secure passwords, allowing you to maintain unique passwords without needing to remember each one.

- **Enable Two-Factor Authentication (2FA)**: Two-factor authentication provides an additional layer of security by requiring a second form of verification to access your accounts. Even if someone has your password, they won't be able to log in without the second factor. 2FA options include:

- SMS Codes: A code sent to your phone via text message.
- Authenticator Apps: Apps like Google Authenticator or Authy generate time-sensitive codes for logging in.
- Biometric Verification: Using fingerprints or facial recognition for added security on supported devices.

Enable 2FA on essential accounts like email, banking, and social media to enhance protection against unauthorized access.

Managing Data Permissions

Many apps request access to various types of data on your device, like location, contacts, or camera. Managing these permissions helps control what personal information apps can access, reducing privacy risks.

- **Review Data Permissions Regularly**: It's essential to check app permissions periodically, especially after updates or when installing new apps. Go to your device's privacy settings to view and adjust permissions:
  - **iOS**: Go to **Settings** > **Privacy** to see a list of permissions by type (e.g., Location Services, Contacts, Camera). You can review and control which apps have access to each category.
  - **Android**: Open **Settings** > **Privacy** > **Permission Manager** (or **Settings** > **Apps** > **Permissions** on some devices). You can see all permissions and which apps are using them, then adjust access for each app.
- **Limit Permissions to What's Necessary**: Only grant permissions that are essential for the app's function. For

example, a weather app may need access to your location for accurate forecasting, but a photo editing app doesn't need access to your contacts. Deny or revoke permissions that seem unnecessary or intrusive.

- **Use "Allow Once" or "Only While Using" Options****: Some devices allow you to set permissions to "Allow Once" or "Only While Using the App," which prevents apps from accessing your data in the background. This can help improve both security and battery life.

Tips for Staying Secure Online

Beyond passwords and permissions, practicing safe online habits is essential for protecting yourself from security threats like phishing attacks and malware.

- **Be Cautious of Phishing Emails and Messages**: Phishing is a common scam where attackers impersonate trusted sources to steal personal information. To avoid phishing attacks:
    - o **Verify the Sender**: Check the sender's email address or phone number for accuracy. Phishing messages often come from addresses with slight misspellings or unusual domains.
    - o **Avoid Clicking on Suspicious Links**: Hover over links to see where they lead before clicking. Phishing emails often contain links that look legitimate but lead to fake login pages.
    - o **Never Provide Personal Information**: Legitimate companies will not ask for sensitive information, like passwords or credit card details, via email. If you receive a suspicious message, contact the organization directly to verify its authenticity.
- **Regularly Update Software and Apps**: Software updates often include important security patches that protect against known vulnerabilities. By keeping your device's operating

system, apps, and browser up to date, you reduce the risk of malware or data breaches. Here's how to manage updates:

- o **Enable Automatic Updates**: Most devices allow you to turn on automatic updates for apps and operating systems, so you receive the latest security improvements without manual intervention.
- o **Check for Updates Manually**: Occasionally check for updates on your devices, especially if you have disabled automatic updates.
  - **iOS**: Go to **Settings** > **General** > **Software Update** to see if your iPhone has the latest version.
  - **Android**: Open **Settings** > **System** > **System Update** to manually check for updates.

- **Use Secure Networks**: Avoid using public Wi-Fi for sensitive activities, like online banking or shopping, as it may be more vulnerable to attacks. When on public networks, consider using a **Virtual Private Network (VPN)** to encrypt your internet connection, adding an extra layer of security.
- **Clear Browser Cache and Cookies**: Regularly clearing your browser's cache and cookies helps protect your personal information and reduces tracking by websites. This practice also prevents stored login data from being accessed if someone gains access to your device.

Summary of Basic Security Steps

Taking proactive steps to secure your online accounts and data— like using strong passwords, managing app permissions, and staying cautious of phishing—greatly reduces the risk of security breaches. By enabling two-factor authentication, updating software regularly, and carefully monitoring app permissions, you strengthen your defenses against hackers and ensure a safer, more private online experience. Consistently practicing these habits can help you maintain control over your personal information and digital presence.

17. Common Troubleshooting Tips for AI Devices

Simple Solutions to Common Problems

When encountering issues with devices or apps, simple troubleshooting steps often resolve the problem quickly. Restarting devices, checking for updates, ensuring network connections, and retraining voice recognition are basic solutions that can fix a range of issues without requiring advanced technical knowledge.

Quick Fixes for Common Issues

- **Restart Your Device if It's Unresponsive**: Restarting is a quick and effective way to resolve issues like freezing, lagging, or apps not loading properly. Restarting clears temporary files, frees up memory, and closes background processes that might be causing slowdowns or unresponsiveness.
    - **How to Restart**:
        - On most smartphones and tablets, hold down the power button and select "Restart" or "Power Off."
        - For computers, click the "Restart" option from the power menu.
    - **Benefits**: Restarting can refresh system performance and often resolves minor glitches, giving you a clean slate.
- **Check for Updates in the App Store**: Software updates for apps and operating systems frequently include bug fixes, performance improvements, and security patches.
    - **Updating Apps**:
        - **iOS**: Open the **App Store**, tap on your profile icon, scroll to the "Available Updates" section, and select "Update All" to get the latest versions of your apps.

- **Android**: Open **Google Play Store**, go to "My Apps & Games," and tap "Update All" to install available updates.
  - **Updating the Device's Operating System**: Keeping your operating system current reduces the chances of issues caused by compatibility problems. Go to your device's settings (e.g., **Settings** > **System** > **Software Update**) and check for updates regularly.

Troubleshooting Voice Assistants

Voice assistants like Siri, Google Assistant, and Alexa can occasionally experience issues with responding accurately. Here are simple steps to troubleshoot common voice assistant problems:

- **Ensure the Device is Connected to Wi-Fi**: Most voice assistants require an active internet connection to process requests and provide responses. If your device is having trouble connecting, check your Wi-Fi settings:
  - **Reconnect to Wi-Fi**: Go to **Settings** > **Wi-Fi** on your device, make sure it's connected, and test with another app to verify the connection.
  - **Restart the Router**: If the Wi-Fi connection is unstable, try restarting your router by unplugging it for about 10 seconds, then plugging it back in. This often resolves connectivity issues and may improve the voice assistant's response times.
- **Re-train the Voice Recognition**: If the voice assistant isn't recognizing your voice properly or responding accurately, re-training its voice recognition can improve performance. Here's how to re-train each major voice assistant:
  - **Siri**: On an iPhone, go to **Settings** > **Siri & Search** > **Listen for "Hey Siri"** > **Set Up "Hey Siri"**. Follow the prompts to re-train Siri to recognize your voice.

- o **Google Assistant**: Open the **Google Assistant** app, tap on your profile picture, go to **Assistant Settings > Voice Match**, and select **Teach Your Assistant Your Voice Again**.
- o **Alexa**: Open the **Alexa** app, tap **Settings > Alexa Account > Recognized Voices > Your Voice** and follow the prompts to re-train Alexa.

Re-training voice recognition helps the assistant understand your unique speech patterns, improving response accuracy and reducing misinterpretations.

Resources for Further Help

If basic troubleshooting steps don't resolve the issue, several resources can provide additional help:

- **Manufacturer Support Websites**: Most tech companies have detailed support websites that offer troubleshooting guides, FAQs, and even live chat or call options to assist with more complex issues.
  - o **Apple Support**: **support.apple.com** provides step-by-step guides, video tutorials, and online forums for iPhones, Macs, iPads, and more.
  - o **Google Support**: **support.google.com** has resources for Google Assistant, Android, Chromebooks, and other Google products.
  - o **Amazon Support**: **support.amazon.com** offers help with Alexa, Kindle, and Fire devices, with FAQs and troubleshooting advice.
- **YouTube Tutorials**: YouTube is a valuable resource for visual learners, offering numerous video tutorials that provide step-by-step guidance on fixing common issues with various devices and software.
  - o **Device-Specific Tutorials**: Search for your device model and issue on YouTube (e.g., "iPhone 12 not

responding" or "re-train Alexa voice recognition") to find video guides from tech experts.

- o **Software Tips and Tricks**: Channels like Tech Insider, CNET, and HowToGeek regularly post tutorials covering troubleshooting tips, app updates, and new features for major operating systems and apps.

Summary of Troubleshooting Steps

Addressing common tech issues is often a matter of following basic troubleshooting steps, like restarting your device, checking for updates, verifying Wi-Fi connections, and re-training voice recognition. These solutions can solve many problems without needing technical assistance. For more complex issues, manufacturer support websites and YouTube tutorials provide in-depth guidance, helping users navigate and resolve problems effectively. Taking advantage of these simple solutions and resources ensures a smoother, more reliable experience with your devices.

18. The Future of AI: What's Next?

Upcoming AI Technologies

AI technology is advancing rapidly, and it's set to become even more deeply integrated into our everyday lives, making routine tasks easier, enhancing health management, and offering more personalized experiences. The upcoming AI trends and innovations will impact a wide range of areas, including healthcare, home automation, and personal assistants, transforming how we interact with devices, manage our well-being, and connect with others.

Key Areas of AI Integration

- **Everyday Devices**: AI is being embedded in devices we use daily, such as smartphones, wearables, home appliances, and even cars. These devices will become smarter and more intuitive, learning from user habits to offer customized suggestions, streamline tasks, and proactively address user needs.
- **Healthcare**: AI advancements in healthcare are set to bring major improvements in diagnostics, treatment, and preventive care. We can expect further development in AI-driven tools for monitoring vital signs, detecting early symptoms of chronic conditions, and supporting telemedicine for more accessible and accurate healthcare.
- **Home Automation**: As AI-powered home automation systems evolve, smart homes will become more integrated and responsive to users' routines. Voice-activated devices, automated lighting, temperature control, security systems, and even kitchen appliances will work together seamlessly, creating an environment that adapts to users' preferences and daily patterns.
- **Personal Assistants**: AI-driven personal assistants like Siri, Google Assistant, and Alexa will grow more capable,

understanding context better, responding with more natural language, and managing a broader range of tasks. These assistants will move toward a more conversational, human-like interaction style, making them easier and more intuitive for users of all ages.

How AI Might Evolve

The evolution of AI promises more tailored, accessible, and user-friendly experiences. Here's a look at some anticipated developments:

- **More Personalized Experiences**: Future AI systems will leverage advanced machine learning algorithms to analyze user behavior, preferences, and needs in greater detail. Personalized recommendations and suggestions will not only reflect general preferences but also adapt dynamically to immediate contexts. For example, smart home devices might adjust lighting, music, and temperature based on the user's current mood or schedule, while healthcare apps may offer wellness advice tailored to individual fitness or health data.
- **Improved Accessibility and Support for Seniors**: AI will play a crucial role in assisting senior users with daily routines, enhancing independence and well-being. Future AI tools will likely feature easier navigation, voice-activated controls, and large, simple interfaces that support seniors in managing health, communicating with family, and controlling home environments. Additionally, voice assistants and smart home devices will become more adaptive, providing reminders, emergency alerts, and real-time support for seniors living alone.

Encouragement to Keep Learning

As AI continues to evolve and become more widespread, embracing these changes is key to making the most of these technologies. Learning about new features, experimenting with different tools, and staying updated on AI developments can help you harness the benefits of these advancements.

- **Embrace New AI Tools**: Many AI tools are designed to simplify tasks, so trying out new features can reveal capabilities that may improve your daily life. For instance, using AI-powered personal finance apps can make budgeting easier, while experimenting with smart home settings can improve comfort and energy efficiency.
- **Stay Curious and Explore New Features**: Many devices now offer built-in tutorials or tips for exploring new functionalities. Don't hesitate to try these features or experiment with different settings. Exploration helps build confidence and familiarity, and it's the best way to uncover features that may not be immediately apparent.
- **Look Out for User-Friendly Innovations**: As AI technology becomes more accessible, many apps and devices are prioritizing simplicity in design, making it easier for all users to adopt these technologies. Explore innovations that provide clear instructions and guided setups, and check out resources like YouTube or device manuals to deepen your understanding.

Summary of Upcoming AI Developments

AI is rapidly advancing, with upcoming technologies expected to make everyday devices smarter, enhance healthcare, and improve personal assistants. As these tools become increasingly personalized and user-friendly, especially for seniors, they offer exciting possibilities for streamlining tasks and supporting individual needs. Staying curious and open to exploring these new tools allows you to leverage AI's potential, keeping you informed and empowered to make the most of each new feature. By embracing AI as it evolves, you can enjoy a more connected, convenient, and customized experience.

19. FAQs: Common Questions

AI has become a helpful and accessible tool in daily life, from managing tasks with voice assistants to staying in touch with family and friends. However, as with any technology, understanding how to use it safely and effectively can make a significant difference. Here are some common questions about using AI and tips on maximizing its benefits.

Q: Is AI safe to use?

A: Yes, AI is generally safe to use, especially when you take steps to secure your personal information. However, AI applications collect data to personalize experiences, so it's essential to be mindful of privacy settings and choose trusted apps from reputable developers.

- **Manage Privacy Settings**: Go to your app or device's privacy settings to control what data is shared, such as location, contacts, or browsing activity. Many apps allow you to limit data access or customize permissions for greater privacy.
- **Use Secure Accounts**: Always secure your accounts with strong, unique passwords and enable two-factor authentication (2FA) where possible. This adds an extra layer of security, especially for sensitive information on finance, health, or personal identity apps.
- **Download from Trusted Sources**: Only install AI-powered apps from official app stores (like the App Store or Google Play) or from trusted companies. Check reviews and permissions to ensure the app aligns with your security needs.

By taking these steps, you can enjoy the convenience of AI while keeping your personal information secure.

Q: What if I can't get the voice assistant to work?

A: If your voice assistant isn't responding, several troubleshooting steps can help restore its functionality. Here's a checklist to ensure everything is set up correctly:

- **Check Wi-Fi or Network Connection**: Voice assistants require an internet connection to process requests. Go to **Settings** on your device and verify that it's connected to Wi-Fi or a mobile network. If connectivity issues persist, restart your router or reconnect to Wi-Fi.
- **Ensure the Voice Assistant Is Enabled**: Go to your device settings to check if the assistant is enabled. For example:
  - **Siri**: Go to **Settings** > **Siri & Search** and toggle **Listen for "Hey Siri"** on.
  - **Google Assistant**: Open the Google Assistant app, tap your profile picture, go to **Assistant Settings**, and confirm that Voice Match is on.
- **Re-train Voice Recognition**: If the assistant struggles to recognize your voice, re-train the voice recognition:
  - **Siri**: In **Settings** > **Siri & Search**, choose **Set Up "Hey Siri"** to re-train it.
  - **Google Assistant**: Open the app, go to **Assistant Settings** > **Voice Match**, and select **Teach Your Assistant Your Voice Again**.
  - **Alexa**: Open the **Alexa** app, go to **Settings** > **Alexa Account** > **Recognized Voices**, and follow the steps to improve voice recognition.

If these steps don't resolve the issue, refer to the assistant's support website for additional troubleshooting guides.

Q: How can AI help me stay in touch with my family?

A: AI offers a variety of ways to stay connected with family and friends, from video calls and messaging to smart device management. Here are a few convenient options:

- **Video Call Apps**: AI-powered video call apps like **Zoom, Google Meet**, and **FaceTime** make it easy to have face-to-face conversations. These apps use AI to improve video quality, reduce background noise, and support real-time captions, making calls clearer and more accessible.
- **Messaging Apps with AI Features**: Apps like **WhatsApp** and **Messenger** include smart replies and suggestions for quick responses, making it easy to stay in touch with minimal typing. They also offer image and video sharing, which AI can enhance by adjusting lighting, optimizing clarity, and adding effects.
- **Voice Commands for Calls and Messages**: AI assistants allow you to make calls or send messages hands-free. For example:
    - **"Hey Siri, call Mom"** or **"Hey Google, message Dad on WhatsApp"** lets you reach family members with just your voice.
    - Alexa can also make calls or drop in on compatible Alexa-enabled devices within the same household, enabling family members to stay connected with ease.

Whether it's a quick call, a shared photo, or a scheduled reminder to connect, AI simplifies communication and helps you stay close to loved ones no matter where they are.

Final Tips

Embracing AI tools can simplify daily routines, enhance safety, and strengthen connections with family and friends. If you're new to AI, don't hesitate to explore different features—AI technology is designed to be user-friendly, and experimenting with it can reveal surprising benefits and capabilities. By managing privacy settings, learning basic troubleshooting, and using AI features for communication, you can enjoy a more connected, convenient, and secure experience.

20. Conclusion and Encouragement to Keep Exploring AI

Recap of Key Points

AI technology has quickly become an integral part of daily life, offering tools that simplify tasks, enhance productivity, and improve our ability to connect with others. From organizing schedules to exploring new hobbies, AI is accessible, user-friendly, and adaptable to individual needs. Here are some key takeaways:

- **AI as a Daily Tool**: AI-powered tools like voice assistants, smart devices, and learning apps offer a range of practical functions, from setting reminders and managing home automation to recommending personalized content and facilitating online learning. These tools make everyday tasks more efficient, freeing up time for other priorities.
- **Versatility in Applications**: AI applications span across various areas—health, finance, communication, learning, and safety—providing solutions that cater to diverse needs. For example, AI can help track health metrics, manage finances through budgeting apps, and keep you connected with family through smart messaging and video call features.
- **User-Friendly Design**: AI tools are designed with ease of use in mind, making them accessible to a broad audience, including seniors and beginners. With features like simple voice commands, personalized suggestions, and intuitive app layouts, AI supports people of all skill levels and technological backgrounds.

Keep Exploring AI

The possibilities of AI are vast, and it's a field that's constantly evolving. Staying curious and open to exploring new features and apps can help you get the most out of these tools and discover new ways to simplify or enhance your life.

- **Experiment with New Apps and Features**: Don't hesitate to try out AI-powered apps or enable new features on your existing devices. Many AI tools are designed for trial and exploration, allowing you to adjust settings, test new functionalities, and personalize them to suit your lifestyle. For instance:
    - Try using AI-powered task management apps to improve productivity.
    - Explore voice assistant skills to automate routines or set custom reminders.
    - Use AI-driven recommendation systems to discover music, books, or online courses you might enjoy.
- **Stay Updated on AI Developments**: AI technology is advancing rapidly, with regular updates, new apps, and emerging tools. Staying informed about these developments helps you take advantage of the latest improvements. Sign up for tech newsletters, follow reliable sources for AI news, or subscribe to technology-focused YouTube channels to stay in the loop.

Resources for Further Learning

Whether you're new to AI or want to deepen your understanding, numerous resources can help you learn how to use AI tools effectively:

- **TechBoomers**: TechBoomers is an excellent online resource offering beginner-friendly tutorials on popular apps, including AI-powered ones. It provides clear, step-by-step guides covering essential features and functionalities for users of all skill levels.
- **YouTube Tutorials**: YouTube is a valuable resource for visual learners, with countless videos on AI basics,

troubleshooting, and specific app guides. Channels like Tech Insider, HowToGeek, and CNET often cover the latest AI tools, sharing tips, demonstrations, and reviews to help you make the most of new features.

- **Community Classes and Libraries**: Many local libraries, community centers, and adult education programs offer classes on technology, including sessions on AI tools and applications. These classes are often hands-on, allowing you to get personalized guidance and explore AI features in a supportive environment.

Embrace AI as a Learning Journey

AI is an exciting and dynamic field that offers endless opportunities for learning and personal growth. By staying open to experimentation and using available resources, you can continue discovering new ways to leverage AI in your daily life, making routines smoother, tasks easier, and interactions more meaningful. Each new skill or feature explored brings you closer to fully embracing the benefits AI offers, creating a more connected, efficient, and enjoyable life experience.

www.ingramcontent.com/pod-product-compliance
Lightning Source LLC
Chambersburg PA
CBHW071304050326
40690CB00011B/2519